HARDBALL

Victoria Stewart

I0139764

BROADWAY PLAY PUBLISHING INC
New York
www.broadwayplaypublishing.com
info@broadwayplaypublishing.com

HARDBALL
© Copyright 2018 Victoria Stewart

First edition: June 2018
I S B N: 978-0-88145-774-2

Book design: Marie Donovan
Page make-up: Adobe InDesign
Typeface: Palatino

HARDBALL was developed with support from the Helen Merrill Award, The Playwrights' Center's Jerome Fellowship Program, the Donmar Warehouse, Hartford Stage, City Theater, Vineyard Theater, Northlight Theater, the Pittsburgh Public Theater, SPF 2006 and the 2005 Women Playwrights Festival co-produced by Seattle Repertory Theatre and Hedgebrook.

HARDBALL premiered at Live Girls! Theater in Seattle in 2011. The cast and creative contributors were:

VIRGINIA	Jaime Roberts
IRENE	Jill Snyder
JIM	Roy Stanton
DANIEL	Shawn Belyea
PAT	Shawnmarie Stanton
SUZANNE	Alyssa Keene
Director	MeghanShalom Arnette
Set design & construction	Brian Stricklan
Lighting design	Melinda Short
Video design	Michael Lindgren
Costume design	Michele Hallman
Sound design/Original music	Erin Stewart
Stage manager/Props design	Meggan Davis
Stage manager/Props design	Alison Underdahl

HARDBALL was the winner of the 2007 Francesca Primus Award and a finalist for the 2008 Susan Smith Blackburn Award.

CHARACTERS & SETTING

VIRGINIA EAMES, *charming, funny, very pretty, political pundit, late 20s/30s. Hardworking, but things have come easily for her.*

JIM LAUDERDALE, *political advisor, consummate pro, maybe a trace of a Southern accent, late 50s/early 60s. A bulldog, but with a sense of sorrow at how things have turned out.*

DANIEL CAMERON, *Editor of a major metropolitan newspaper, 50s. Attractive older man, integrity personified, weary, George Plimptonesque.*

PAT MORSE, *Assistant Editor of the same newspaper, late 40s/50s. Dry, witty, sharp, brittle but always right.*

IRENE SHAY, *capable, efficient newscaster, mid 40s.*

SUZANNE ROTH, *the wife of an American journalist, 30s.*

Time: The play begins in early February 2005, the beginning of Bush's 2nd term as President.

While the characters of this play are meant to mirror personalities in political life today, HARDBALL is a work of fiction.

Notes on the set: The set should be flexible but a prominent feature needs to be the use of the video. The video needs to be inescapable fact of the landscape. The screens should either be embedded in the set or the video could be projected using a rear projection screen.

Notes on text: Slashes "/" indicate that the text should overlap.

We should invade their countries, kill their leaders and convert them to Christianity. We weren't punctilious about locating and punishing only Hitler and his top officers. We carpet-bombed German cities; we killed civilians. That's war. And this is war.
Ann Coulter, *National Review,* 9/13/01

T V's a little strange, isn't it? A tiny lit-up twisted replica of everything, that's trying to eliminate our world, and take its place.
Len Jenkin, *American Notes*

all alone by a barren well,
scarecrow's only scarin' himself.
Beck, *Guero*

ACT ONE

Prologue
Virginia, a different kind of American, has a conversation with herself.

(VIRGINIA in her apartment. She sets up a videocamera in front of her.)

(She looks into it. We see her face in close up on a T V screen. She peers at herself, gets up, adjusts the camera, sits back down. Frames herself in the video monitor. She cricks her neck, shakes her hands out. She's keyed up and excited.)

(She looks at a sheet of paper in her lap. She's amusing herself—she pauses as if being interviewed—she is being her most charming self-confident self.)

VIRGINIA: Well, Ms Shay, thank you so much for having me on *The Press Speaks*.

(As if she's answering a question)

It started as a joke really.

I worked at *The Post* for six years, started there as an intern, you know? And during the presidential election, tensions at the paper are high.

It's a close race and we're not supposed to admit for whom we're voting because we're reporters, we're "objective", right? So here I am, trying really hard to be "objective" but when we're at the bar after work, it's clear everyone in the office is voting for the bland kept military poseur that is Kerry.

I mean, who are we kidding? The man has the
charisma of Al Gore, but without the sex appeal.
(She smiles wickedly.)
Without the *sizzle*.
After a couple of drinks, people are doing bad
imitations of G W and someone says, "Those red
neck hicks, they just don't know any better. As if the
terrorists are planning to attack their *trailer parks*."
It got to me, you know? Because I'm not a red neck
hick.
I went to a good school.
I drink merlot.
But that's the thing—all of my co-workers feel that
if Republicans are somehow different from them, a
different species—they don't have to listen to them.
So I say to this friend of mine, who's kind of my boss—
was anyway—that I should wear a Bush pin to work,
just to show them that somebody they actually *work
with* is planning to vote for Bush. He laughs nervously
and basically bans me from doing it.
(Her joking façade drops for a moment.)
There's more to it than that. There's something about
the look he gives me. I can see in that moment that…
that he feels sorry for me.
(Back to façade, in a stand-up comedy voice) "A Democrat
and a Republican walk into a bar and the bartender
says, 'what is this, a *joke*?'"
Have you heard that one?
So I decide to put my friend to the test.
The next day, I wear the Bush pin as sort of a "mind
fuck"—
(Out of the character) Can say I "fuck"? It is cable…
—Sort of a prank. Between us.
But over the course of the day, —um—the scales fall
from my eyes. Everybody, all these people I have

worked with for years treat me with complete disdain.
All these people who supposedly are more open, more
accepting. Nothing shocks *them*, right?

These are people who think that the terrorists who
attacked us on 9/11 are merely misunderstood
waifs who need counseling and a big hug but me,
acknowledging that I'm planning to vote Republican—
this, they can't accept.

I'm a pariah. Suddenly, I understood what Dennis
Kucinich's high school years must have been like.

(An interviewer response)

That's what *I* said, Ms Shay.

Oh, *Irene*, sure, I knew you'd understand.

My friend brings me into his office and reads me the
policy. And it's mortifying, like the principal's office,
you know?

I know what I'm *supposed* to do, meekly take off my
pin, and get back to work. But I don't. I have a blog,
that I set up when I was in grad school, virginiaeames.
com and I start a countdown on it, thinking I'll count
the days, how long I get away with it.

(A sly smile)

I'm always trying to get away with something.

I wear the pin in on Monday and by nine o'clock, I'm
packing my desk.

(A response to the interviewer)

Honestly, Irene, I never thought I'd be fired for my
political beliefs.

(Response)

I *am* glad I spoke up. Freedom of speech is one of our
founding freedoms. The right to speak, the right to be
heard. That's why I became a JOURNALIST.

But as a Republican journalist, I'm supposed to *obscure*
my beliefs in these strange, convoluted ways. I'm
supposed to pretend I'm something I'm not.

And I will not lie. I am who I am.

I've learned that about myself.

(Conspiratorially) And I've also learned that Democrats just do *not* know how to take a joke.

(She smiles into the camera.)

Scene One
Affirmative Action:
Virginia takes the first step and falters.

(A T V studio. VIRGINIA *slowly and uncertainly makes her way to the sound stage with three chairs. She is wearing a suit with a very short skirt and high heels.* IRENE, *a very polished T V journalist, enters, walking briskly.)*

IRENE: *(Talking to herself)* I can't believe you said that!

VIRGINIA: Ms Shay? Irene?

IRENE: *(Laughing)* Don't make me come up there, you son of a bitch.

VIRGINIA: What?

*(*IRENE *sees* VIRGINIA.*)*

IRENE: *(Gesturing to her earpiece, explaining)* Not you. Bob, my producer.

And you are...?

VIRGINIA: Virginia. Virginia Eames.

IRENE: Thrilled you could make it on such short notice.

VIRGINIA: I watch your show religiously—Your interview with Tom Delay was—

IRENE: *(Gesturing to a chair)* You're there.

(To her producer) Whaddya mean, she's not giving interviews?

VIRGINIA: What? / Oh.

IRENE: *(Ignoring* VIRGINIA*)* Pulease, everyone gives interviews.

Let's send her something—
What says, "Your husband's a hostage, good luck with that, and by the way, give us an exclusive interview." No, we can't send her *flowers,* her husband's not dead yet. What's wrong with you, let's send her a tuna casserole while we're at it, a wreath of *lilies*—
A fruit basket? The Today show sent her a fruit basket the size of Brazil.
Oo, she likes Frangelico? Where'd you hear that? Mark goes to her *synagogue*? Are you fucking kidding me? Why am I talking to you and not talking to Mark? Fine, we'll send the fruit basket from Mark, like he's a concerned friend or something.
He *is* a concerned friend? Look, you bastard, I'm concerned about whether we're getting this fucking interview so send the fruit basket TODAY.
(Clipped) Yeah. Love you too.

VIRGINIA: So are we—

IRENE: What?

VIRGINIA: Going to go over the—story, whatever.

IRENE: It's your story, right? You know what happened. So tell me.

VIRGINIA: It all started—

IRENE: Not now. On T V.

*(*VIRGINIA *notices the other chair.)*

VIRGINIA: Uh—yes. Is there another guest?

IRENE: Jim Lauderdale.

VIRGINIA: Wow.

IRENE: The intern didn't tell you? Kristen?

VIRGINIA: Cathy?

IRENE: Whatever her name is, she didn't tell you?

VIRGINIA: No.

IRENE: What did she say?

VIRGINIA: That it was an interview.

IRENE: An interview with you is going to take, what—a minute— "wow, you were fired?" and we have fifteen to fill so…

VIRGINIA: Oh.

IRENE: The show's about "Bias." God, am I sick of talking about *(Air quotes)* "BIAS." I mean, it's not like there isn't NEWS to report.
Is there a problem?

VIRGINIA: No, I just wish I had—

IRENE: *(To her producer)* Bob, Virginia was under the impression we were only talking about her and now she's looking like a deer in headlights. Can we get her an epinephrine shot?
(Gestures to VIRGINIA, *"I'm kidding")*
And can we PLEASE do something about Kristen, Cathy, whatever her name is, she has the mental acuity of cat litter.
I know she's Shelton's niece but…Uhhuh—uh huh—
(To VIRGINIA*)* She's fired.

VIRGINIA: Oh no, I didn't—

IRENE: I'm lying. We couldn't get rid of her even if she set the greenroom on fire.

VIRGINIA: Good.

IRENE: We keep leaving her behind on station retreats and she keeps finding her way back. Damn her sense of direction.

VIRGINIA: Okay.

IRENE: I apologize. Misinformation is the rule of the day. But you were on debate club, right?

VIRGINIA: No.

IRENE: *(Taking in the short skirt and heels)* You were a cheerleader, am I right.

VIRGINIA: Um…yeah.

IRENE: *(Dryly)* Go Wildcats.

VIRGINIA: Bears. Our team were the / Bears….

IRENE: I'm just saying, you can do this. You don't have to be so nervous.

VIRGINIA: I'm not nervous.

IRENE: You don't have to be.

VIRGINIA: I'm not.
(Nervously) I didn't know Jim Lauderdale would be here. That's why I'm a little *(She gestures with her hands.)* "aah!"

IRENE: Since you're an unknown quantity, we wanted a ringer, a—

VIRGINIA: A known quantity.

IRENE: Yes.

VIRGINIA: Jim Lauderdale, heady company.

IRENE: I saw your tape. You'll be fine. And Jim's… Jim's a pussycat. Once you get to know him.

(JIM enters.)

JIM: Irene.

IRENE: Jim.

(JIM and Irene kiss each other's cheek.)

IRENE: Jim. Virginia Eames.

JIM: I've been reading your blog. Virginiaeames.com, right?

VIRGINIA: You read my blog?

JIM: I read everything, sugar.

VIRGINIA: I saw you speak at the College Repub—

(Music begins.)

IRENE: We're about to start.

JIM: Do I have anything between my teeth, Virginia?

VIRGINIA: No—

JIM: The hair? The hair's okay, what's left?

(JIM grins at VIRGINIA. *The music swells and the lights change.)*

IRENE: This is Irene Shay and welcome to *The Press Speaks*. We're here to discuss the always relevant topic of media bias. Our guests are Virginia Eames who was fired from her job at *The Post* for wearing a "Vote for Bush" pin during the 2004 election and Jim Lauderdale, a consultant for several political campaigns.
Mr Lauderdale, how would you like to address the issue?

JIM: Well, Ms Shay, we've seen a bias in the media for years. And it affects everything we watch, all the news we consume. It's not even a question anymore. Perhaps the most famous statistic is the Freedom Forum Poll in 1996, eighty-nine percent of reporters voted for Bill Clinton. How are we to take that if not some sort of bias?

IRENE: Ms Eames.

VIRGINIA: Um, just to be completely, you know, specific, it was actually eighty-nine percent of correspondents in Washington D C.

JIM: That's what I said.

VIRGINIA: No, you didn't. Actually.

IRENE: As a member of the Fourth Estate, what's your take on the topic, Ms Eames?

VIRGINIA: Besides that small quibble over details, I completely agree with Mr Lauderdale.

(An uncomfortable pause while JIM *and* IRENE *look at* VIRGINIA *waiting for her to speak.)*

VIRGINIA: Um, well, if you take my own firing as an example, I wore a "vote for Bush" pin and lost my job.

IRENE: But that was the policy, wasn't it? No political pins at the paper, at all. And you were informed in a memo weeks earlier, isn't that correct?

VIRGINIA: Sure—

IRENE: And in fact, that same paper fired two copy editors for going to a Move On fundraiser during the same election.

VIRGINIA: Yes, but what I'm trying to say, to agree with Mr Lauderdale, is why *can't* our politics enter into our jobs—wouldn't it be better just to be truthful, to put our cards on the table and let the American people be the judge.

JIM: Sure, right. But any mainstream journalist has no idea how to tell the truth, that's the problem.

VIRGINIA: Mr Lauderdale is exaggerating.

JIM: No, Ms Eames, I'm not.

VIRGINIA: Journalists enter the profession with extensive training to—

JIM: Training? Look at Jayson Blair. He hadn't even finished college when he was hired by the New York Times.

IRENE: But Blair was *fired* once they discovered that he had plagiarized articles.

JIM: Plagiarized? He just made them up out of whole cloth!

VIRGINIA: To tar *The New York Times* with the same brush just because one reporter happened to be a pathological liar, it's not—I mean, I may not like *The Times*'s Op-Ed page but I wouldn't say—

JIM: And how did he get that job? Liberalism, affirmative action.

IRENE: Blaming Jayson Blair on affirmative action is an oversimplification—

JIM: How else did he stay at that paper for years without affirmative action? The Executive Editor of *The New York Times* admitted that his decision not to listen to all the complaints was due to his white guilt—

VIRGINIA: Partially. *The New York Times* is also a huge organization with a thousand employees—

JIM: Are you for affirmative action?

VIRGINIA: Well—

JIM: "Put your cards on the table and let the American people decide," Ginnie.

VIRGINIA: I would say I'm a Colin Powell Republican. You know?
(She starts again) Affirmative action—

JIM: Why don't you say what you mean, "racial preferences."

VIRGINIA: I am saying what I mean. Um—I think rewarding upwardly mobile behavior—

JIM: What I don't like about the affirmative action scheme is that it's what we fought against in the sixties.

VIRGINIA: But we're not here to talk about—

JIM: Choosing one group over the other on the basis of color is what it sounds like to me.

IRENE: Having a diverse workforce on a newspaper is an asset, don't you think, Ms Eames?

VIRGINIA: Right. Integration is what we're trying to achieve. Isn't that the goal?

JIM: Why?

VIRGINIA: What?

JIM: Why are we trying to achieve integration when in fact other cultural groups are trying to differentiate themselves? All I ever hear about is "cultural community" and "accepting diversity." Is that integration?

VIRGINIA: *(Sputtering)* I think people want their news organizations to reflect the population—uh—which seems to me—what -what we're talking about here, in terms of bias—

IRENE: So you're against affirmative action, Mr Lauderdale.

JIM: When American tax dollars are at stake, in governmental jobs, in a state school, and in my news, yes, I am against racial preferences. Unlike Virginia here.

VIRGINIA: I don't—

JIM: Maybe it's the age difference between me and Virginia, but I can still remember a time when water fountains were marked "colored" and "white". And I don't want to see that again.

VIRGINIA: That's the exact opposite of what—

JIM: You want one set of rules for one color and another set for another color.

VIRGINIA: *(Alarmed)* That's not what I'm saying!

JIM: That's exactly what you're saying. I mean, Ginnie, you say you're a Republican and you're willing to lose your job for your beliefs.

VIRGINIA: I am. I did!

JIM: And that's commendable. But then you wanna pat the New York Times on the back for a job well-done. You want to elevate workers merely on the color of their skin. You want to make excuses for the people who fired you—

VIRGINIA: I'm not—

JIM: I mean, it's like hearing an abused wife say she bumped into a door.

VIRGINIA: I—

IRENE: On an international note, before we move back to George in Baghdad, I wanted to ask if you had any comments on Jeffery Roth, the Newsweek journalist who's been kidnapped by Iraqi insurgents. Ms Eames?

VIRGINIA: *(Flailing)* Um…I'm sorry, I'm not up to date on the—

IRENE: Mr Lauderdale, how do you think this will play out?

JIM: A terrible situation. I hope it resolves before the unthinkable happens.

IRENE: And on today's topic, any last words, Ms Eames?

VIRGINIA: About bias or—?

IRENE: It's your time.

VIRGINIA: Um. I think—affirmative action is a progressive / action—

(JIM *makes a noise of disgust.*)

VIRGINIA: It's a *positive* action, uh, moving us forward, you know…?

(VIRGINIA *looks miserably to* IRENE *for help.* IRENE *turns to* JIM.)

IRENE: Mr Lauderdale.

(JIM *smiles and opens his hands in a shrug.*)

JIM: Ginnie, I don't believe in institutionalized racism. I'm old-fashioned that way.

IRENE: Thank you and now we'll go to George in Baghdad.

(*Music plays and lights change.*)

IRENE: Jim, thank you for your time.

JIM: Darlin', I'll always make time for you.

(JIM *gets up and gives his mike to a techie. He stands off to the side, entering information into his palm pilot as he listens to his messages on his cellphone.*)

VIRGINIA: That was—

IRENE: Trial by fire. Sorry.

VIRGINIA: Why did you have me on here to talk about bias when that wasn't the topic?

IRENE: It was the topic but affirmative action must've been on the White House talking points. Jim gets a memo every morning.

(*Still juggling his phone and palm pilot,* JIM *puts a piece of paper into his pocket.*)

VIRGINIA: I just wish I had been able to prepare.

IRENE: Look, this is a twenty-four hours news channel. *The Press Speaks* is the first thing to go on a heavy news day. Take the good stuff, put it on your reel and move on. Thanks again.
(*She speaks to her producer, hand to her ear, as she exits.*)
(*Without malice*) Well, that was a trainwreck.
Bob? Can we get a pineapple in that fruit basket?

(VIRGINIA *approaches* JIM.)

VIRGINIA: Mr Lauderdale?

JIM: Oh, Ms Eames.

VIRGINIA: I don't know what happened up there but—

JIM: I know what happened up there. You wanted to tell your sad story and I wouldn't let you and now you got your panties in a twist.

VIRGINIA: You made a fool of me.

JIM: Darlin', you use a communist term like "progressive action", you make a fool of yourself.

VIRGINIA: But we were on the *same side*.

JIM: You think they invite people on T V to be on the same side?
(Pointing to himself) Point.
(Pointing to her) Counterpoint. You give me an opening, you sputter and prevaricate, you backtrack, I bury you. That's the way the game is played.

VIRGINIA: *(Fighting tears)* You didn't even give me a chance.

JIM: Miss Eames, stop trying to argue with your short skirt and your four-foot long legs and start using your head. Camera shot ends at your waist, honey.
(He exits.)

Scene Two
At all costs: Daniel makes Virginia an offer.

(DANIEL *and* PAT *sit eating sandwiches in his office. He turns off the T V they had just been watching.)*

PAT: Do you know him? The kidnapped reporter.

DANIEL: Never crossed paths.

PAT: He's got a three year-old girl. Michael at the City desk went to Missouri with him.

DANIEL: Glad I'm stateside.

PAT: Me too.

DANIEL: Virginia, she wasn't so bad.

PAT: Grim.

DANIEL: She looked good.

PAT: Of course, she *looked* good. She always *looks* good. She *sounded*, unfortunately, like an idiot.

DANIEL: It could've been worse.

PAT: How, Daniel, how could it have been any worse?

DANIEL: She could've fallen off her chair.

PAT: You're enjoying this.

DANIEL: No, I'm not.

PAT: Admit it.

DANIEL: A little.

(DANIEL *eats his sandwich. Shrugs.* PAT *looks at him but then looks down at her sandwich.*)

PAT: She's not coming back.

(DANIEL *looks up from his sandwich.* PAT*'s giving her lunch considerable attention.*)

PAT: To the paper. I know you think now she's failed so she'll come running back to us here at *The Post* but she's not.

DANIEL: (*Not looking at her*) I know she's not.

PAT: You're not allowed to suggest it.

DANIEL: Pat—

PAT: You're not allowed. She's a big girl. She can make her own decisions.

DANIEL: But it's a *mistake*.

PAT: Do you think that I like that she got herself fired just so she could write about it on her *"blog?"* I do not.

DANIEL: I tried to stop her—

PAT: And she didn't listen to you then.

DANIEL: No.

PAT: She wanted to leave the paper. She found a way to do it that would make her look like a martyr and give her some press. So you're not allowed to even suggest working here again.

DANIEL: I did not teach her everything I know so she could write for a *website*.

PAT: She doesn't want to be a journalist, she wants to be on T V. Let her.

DANIEL: But she was awful.

PAT: Well, what does she have to *say*? She wanted her own column. Why any person under thirty needs their own column is beyond me.

DANIEL: She gives good demographic.

(DANIEL *and* PAT *eat silently. She gets up and looks out the window.*)

PAT: I blame Clinton.

DANIEL: For what?

PAT: Everything.

DANIEL: Can you be more specific?

PAT: We just saw some reporter kidnapped and in danger because of Clinton—

DANIEL: Because of Bush.

PAT: No, because of Clinton. Do you think we would be in Iraq right now if Gore won four years ago? No. Clinton sacrificed everything, his legacy, the

Democrats, the Middle East, all because he had to be fellated in the Oval Office.

DANIEL: I don't think I've ever heard you use that word.

PAT: What, "oval"?

DANIEL: Ha, ha.

PAT: Watching the inauguration last week, I realized how furious I was. If Gore had won, we would've had eight very peaceful, very boring years.

DANIEL: "May you live in uninteresting times."

PAT: What?

DANIEL: You know, that Chinese proverb. Someone sent it to me after 9/11.

PAT: What I wouldn't give for uninteresting times.

DANIEL: We thought Reaganism was the end of everything. It wasn't.

PAT: Right, and then Clinton rolled back two terms of progress for an orgasm.

DANIEL: I think it was more than one.

PAT: Does that make it worth it?

DANIEL: Desire's a funny thing.

PAT: Oh, is that what it is? Is that what you call it, *desire*?

DANIEL: "You"? So now, I'm among / the bad guys.

PAT: *(Overlapping)* Yes, Men in general, yes maybe. No one's explained it to me in a way that I understand.

DANIEL: Well, if you don't understand it, I can't explain it.

PAT: Daniel. Don't ask her to come back. It'll look—

DANIEL: I won't.

What does *that* mean?

PAT: What?

DANIEL: "It'll look——" What does that mean?

PAT: We have to be consistent.

DANIEL: You don't think I'm consistent?

(VIRGINIA *is in the doorway.*)

VIRGINIA: Hey guys.

PAT/DANIEL: Hey…

DANIEL: Weren't you *great*? I'm so proud of you.

(*As* VIRGINIA *enters,* PAT *offers her a tissue box.* VIRGINIA *tries to put on a good face.*)

VIRGINIA: No, I cried in the cab on the way here.

DANIEL: It wasn't that bad.

VIRGINIA: I haven't even seen it and I hate myself.
(*A sudden thought, she puts her head in her hands.*)
Oh my God, I *taped* it. I taped it so I could watch it again tonight.
(*She starts to cry and takes a tissue.*)
I *practiced*. I used my videocamera and sat in my living room saying these stupid answers to these ridiculous questions I made up.
(*She goes into her purse and pulls out the questions.*)
He made me look like an *idiot*.
(*She ferociously tears up the paper.*)
I felt like I was in some thin hallway and there's some guy who wouldn't let me by. I just wanted some TIME.

DANIEL: He's a jerk.

VIRGINIA: *He's good.* I'm not.

DANIEL: He's a bully.

VIRGINIA: (*Angry*) I don't need your pity, okay?

PAT: Then stop asking for it.

DANIEL: Pat…

PAT: No. Virginia, you were thrown by that kidnapped reporter. How could you not know that? It's been all over the news this morning.

VIRGINIA: I was *practicing* all morning, Pat!

PAT: You were uninformed and bland. Where was your wit, your edge?

VIRGINIA: I didn't feel witty.

PAT: That's not an option. Be sharp. Be certain. Be specific. They have to be afraid to cut away from you. Don't you have another piece this week?

VIRGINIA: Just some local commentary show. This was my chance. This was national.

PAT: You have opinions, strong ones, so use them. Do you think a man on that show would've just let Lauderdale roll over him like that?

VIRGINIA: No.

PAT: As a woman, you can't ask for respect. / You have to demand it.

VIRGINIA: You have to demand it, I know…

PAT: Virginia, you're going to have a wonderful career once you get your shit together.

VIRGINIA: *(Affectionately, a little in awe)* You're such a bitch.

PAT: And it's gotten me where I am today.

VIRGINIA: *(Noticing the bottle on the desk)* You guys got champagne…

PAT: To celebrate—

VIRGINIA: —My demise.

PAT: —The loss of your virginity.

DANIEL: Should I leave?

PAT: No, I'll leave and get some glasses.

(PAT *exits*, DANIEL *tries to call her back.*)

DANIEL: Pat, we really shouldn't, we have to get back to—

VIRGINIA: There she goes. *(Pause)* Has anyone claimed responsibility for the kidnapped reporter?

DANIEL: It's all factions now. Nothing you can name.

VIRGINIA: You can always name them.

DANIEL: No one's taken responsibility, that's all I'm saying.

VIRGINIA: It must be so terrifying, to be at risk like that. And all for a story.

DANIEL: For a reporter like him, I think it's worth it.

VIRGINIA: Truth at all costs?

(DANIEL *and* VIRGINIA *smile at each other.*)

VIRGINIA: So how was I, Daniel? Really.

DANIEL: Well, you *looked* great.

(VIRGINIA *rolls her eyes.*)

DANIEL: You know, Virginia, you could always come back...

VIRGINIA: To *The Post*? I don't think so.

DANIEL: We could work it out.

VIRGINIA: I have a column, Daniel.

DANIEL: On a *website*.

VIRGINIA: That's better than *The Post*. They wouldn't give me a column. *You* wouldn't give me a column.

DANIEL: You know I couldn't.

VIRGINIA: You'd print my byline but you wouldn't print my opinions.

DANIEL: Is that so important?

VIRGINIA: I have something to say. My opinions have validity.

DANIEL: I'm not saying they don't.

VIRGINIA: I want people to listen to me. And at *The Post*, no one listens to me.

DANIEL: I listen to you.
(He looks out the door briefly.)

VIRGINIA: Did you ever tell Pat? About us?

DANIEL: No.

VIRGINIA: I wasn't sure.

DANIEL: Why would I tell her?

VIRGINIA: You're close.

DANIEL: If you came back to *The Post*, I could at least see you.

VIRGINIA: That is the point, Daniel. We're not *seeing* each other any more.

DANIEL: Think about it, Virginia.

VIRGINIA: Can we just say it's a career move and leave it at that?

(DANIEL takes out a present, extends it to VIRGINIA.)

DANIEL: Here.

(VIRGINIA doesn't take it.)

DANIEL: It's a gift. A token. Isn't that what they say, a token of my esteem.

(VIRGINIA takes it from DANIEL.)

VIRGINIA: It's your book. It's your book, right.

(DANIEL *walks away from* VIRGINIA. *She unwraps it and reads the inscription.*)

VIRGINIA: "To my helpmate and inspiration."
(She looks at it sadly. She looks up at him.)
Daniel.
Daniel. Look at me.

(DANIEL *turns to* VIRGINIA. PAT *stands in the doorway.*)

PAT: Did you give her a copy of your book, Daniel? A book on Bioterrorism as a going away gift?

(DANIEL *picks up the champagne and unwraps the cap.*)

VIRGINIA: This way he doesn't have to shop.

PAT: What's the inscription, "I'll miss you like I miss smallpox?"

(No one laughs. DANIEL *opens the champagne in silence.)*

PAT: They only had these.
(She produces water cooler cups.)
Remember when they had bras like this?
(She positions the cups on her breasts.)
No, you wouldn't.

DANIEL: Ahem.

(PAT *hands the cups out,* DANIEL *pours.*)

PAT: Toast. To Virginia's ascent. It's only a matter of time.

VIRGINIA: To time.

DANIEL: To time.

Scene Three
Code words: Virginia rewrites.

(VIRGINIA *in her apartment. She looks at a piece of paper on her lap as if memorizing it and jots notes as she makes corrections.)*

VIRGINIA: "Yesterday, one of my own, Jeffery Roth, an American journalist, was kidnapped in Iraq by extremists."
(Corrects herself, out of character) Too bland.
(She mimics PAT.*)*
"Be specific, Virginia."
(She tries this on for size.)
"By Muslim terrorists."
(She pauses, looking into the camera.)
"Jeffery Roth, an American journalist, was kidnapped in Iraq by Muslim terrorists. Not that you'll hear the media call them that. The media—"
No.
(She refines her argument, what would Jim say?)
"*The New York Times* will use code words like "insurgents" or "religious extremists" as if their religion was irrelevant—"
Wait a minute—
(She writes this sentence down.)
"As if the *strength* of their religion superceded their *choice* of religion. The liberal media would like you to believe that fundamentalism of all kinds leads to violence.
Let's compare and contrast, shall we?
During the time that Jeffery Roth was bound, gagged and videotaped for Al Jazeera with a knife to his throat, the Shakers built a couple of *chairs*."
(She stops and muses.)
Baskets, built a couple of baskets?

"Chairs."

(Yeah, that's better.)

"Why is it when a Christian commits a random act of violence, his religion becomes an integral part of the package and yet, when a Muslim commits an act of carnage he's an undefined "religious extremist."

Then again, *The New York Times* considers you a religious extremist if you expect to sing *Jingle Bells* at a public school "holiday" pageant.

Muslims committed the deadliest act of terrorism on American soil and yet when Chechnyans killed a hundred and fifty schoolchildren in Russia, it was mentioned as a parenthetical that the murderers were Muslim."

Hm.

(Correcting herself) "Followed Mohammed."

(She writes "followed Mohammed" down.)

(She looks up into the camera, she's riffing now.)

"Oh, they just *happened* to be Muslim?

Right, and Bill Clinton, the man who put the "moan" in "testimony", just *happened* to be sitting in his Oval office chair when Monica was under his desk with her mouth open.

(She chortles, pleased with herself and writes this.)

Until we are willing to define the perpetrators, how are we supposed to combat them?

(She looks into the camera.)

When we name something, we're that much closer to destroying it."

Scene Four
The kitchen table:
Jeffrey Roth's wife gives one interview.

(On video, an image of a pretty woman in her 30s, an interview at her home. Caption below her image:)
"Suzanne Roth
The wife of Jeffrey Roth, kidnapped reporter."
SUZANNE: Everyone wants to talk to me, I guess because it's good television.
But the only reason why I'm doing this interview is because I know you. You know us, Jeffery and I, and that counts for something.
I'm sorry, I haven't slept in....
In fact, I haven't slept, really slept since he left.
He always leaves in the middle of the night, to get there in the daylight. I'm so used to it, sometimes he doesn't even wake me.
But the last time he did.
A kiss on the cheek, a "be safe, darlin'"
We met at Tulane and he never lost his accent.
(A deep sorrow sets in.)
But this time, I wish—
I wish I had sat with him at our kitchen table while the coffee was brewing.
I wish I had held his hand in mine and said what I never think to say before he leaves.
There are so many things we don't say because saying it would make it too real. The reality of his daily life, when he's there, I never even want to think about. Especially now.
I'm sorry...
(She loses her composure for a moment and then struggles to regain it.)
I know he's coming back to me. I know it.

Because he didn't say goodbye.
(The broadcast ends: Graphics.)

Scene Five
Provocation:
Virginia talks into the void and two friends meet
again.

(DANIEL and VIRGINIA enter a dark satellite studio. There's a single chair and a camera.)

DANIEL: You've never given interviews in a satellite studio before?

VIRGINIA: You know I haven't.

DANIEL: God, it's like a void. Statements in a vacuum. I hate doing this. I like being interviewed by *people.*

VIRGINIA: I'll be interviewed by people, it's just they'll be in California and New York and I'll be here.

DANIEL: And you do this all day.

VIRGINIA: I have—
(She looks at a piece of paper.)
Five. Five interviews today.

DANIEL: All because of one local commentary piece. One piece where you said something provocative.

VIRGINIA: I said the truth.

DANIEL: A fairly bloodthirsty truth.

VIRGINIA: People are responding. People want someone who speaks to them, who doesn't ignore their fear—

DANIEL: *(He ignores this)* Center your chair. See that red light blinking? When it stops flashing, that means, "you're on." When you look into the camera, it'll look like you're looking at the interviewer. But don't be so

fixed or else you look like a robot. Or a "fembot" as
they've been saying lately.

VIRGINIA: *(Brightly)* Ah, you've been reading my press.

DANIEL: Not very flattering.

VIRGINIA: I'm booked all day, two morning shows, one
national, C N N, a whole half-hour on Fox—

DANIEL: Fox's fox.

VIRGINIA: If the shoe fits.

DANIEL: *(Gesturing to her shoes)* Those are new. You
know, the T V can't see those Ferragamos.

(VIRGINIA stiffens a little, remembering JIM's remark.)

VIRGINIA: Where does it cut off?

DANIEL: What?

VIRGINIA: The Camera.

DANIEL: Um. Here.
(He lightly touches her waist.)
On you.
(His hand rests on her hip for a moment.)
Don't you—

VIRGINIA: What?

DANIEL: Have some kind of handler now? Someone
who books you.

VIRGINIA: Yes.

DANIEL: Why didn't you ask him to show you the
ropes?

VIRGINIA: I didn't want to bother him. He has other
clients.

DANIEL: You wanted him to think you had done it
before.

(VIRGINIA is refreshing her make-up.)

VIRGINIA: I *have* done it before.

DANIEL: Not this.

VIRGINIA: You think I can't do it?

DANIEL: I know you can. God, look at you.

(VIRGINIA *looks at* DANIEL.)

VIRGINIA: I'm terrified, Daniel.

DANIEL: I know.

VIRGINIA: You're the only person I can say that to. Who won't use it against me.

DANIEL: Oh come on.

VIRGINIA: You're the one I turn to when I don't know what the fuck I'm doing.
So. Thank you for coming.

DANIEL: I'd do anything for you. You know that.
(He tucks her hair behind her ear.)
You—You need to put your earphone in.

(The moment is broken.)

VIRGINIA: *(Putting in her earphone)* Who taught *you* all this?

DANIEL: George Will. It wasn't as laden with subtext.

VIRGINIA: *(She laughs.)* Daniel—

(JIM *enters.*)

JIM: Ms Eames?

VIRGINIA: Oh. Hi.

JIM: Jim Lauderdale.

VIRGINIA: *(A bit of edge)* I remember.

JIM: I'm in the studio next door and I saw you on the sign in sheet. Thought I'd pay my regards.

DANIEL: Can we help you?

JIM: *(Warmly)* Daniel.

DANIEL: Jim.

JIM: How're sales? Of your book.

DANIEL: Holding steady at about three boxes under my bed.

VIRGINIA: You two know each other?

DANIEL: Jim and I go way back.

JIM: Shame about the book. I recommend it to everyone. World's a scary place once you look at the facts.

DANIEL: I wasn't trying to scare people.

JIM: "Bioterrorism is right around the corner" and you're not trying to scare people?

DANIEL: I think it's important that people think about how precarious the labs are—

JIM: Yeah, yeah, yeah, Fear sells books, Daniel.

DANIEL: Obviously, in my case, it doesn't.

JIM: Aw, you just needed a flashier cover.

VIRGINIA: That's what *I* said.

(DANIEL *gives* VIRGINIA *a dirty look.*)

JIM: Ginnie, I like what you've been saying lately. Incisive.

VIRGINIA: Thank you.

JIM: No, really, we need young people stating their views. What we really need is someone to take on the women. I can't do that. Or I look like a big bully, ain't that right?

VIRGINIA: I'm just telling the truth as I see it.

JIM: It's necessary now. That truth.

VIRGINIA: I agree.

DANIEL: I should—I have to go.

VIRGINIA: Thanks for coming.

DANIEL: We should go and leave Virginia to prepare.

JIM: Ginnie, you don't mind if I watch, do you?

VIRGINIA: What?

JIM: My cab took some quickie route here so I'm thirty minutes early. And they always put these satellites in the worst part of town. There ain't a Starbucks for miles.

(VIRGINIA *looks at* JIM. *Is this a dare?*)

VIRGINIA: Sure.

DANIEL: Do you want me to stay?

VIRGINIA: No. I'll be fine.

(DANIEL *kisses* VIRGINIA *on the cheek.*)

JIM: Good to see you again, Daniel.

(DANIEL *exits.*)

JIM: I like the new you, Ginnie. Suits you better than meek and mild.

VIRGINIA: It's not a new me.

JIM: You're on all the shows advocating racial profiling, I'd say that's a new you.

VIRGINIA: It's not racial / profiling—

JIM: Don't get defensive. I like it. Someone needs to say what you're saying. And a pretty girl, no less. I'm sick of all these dykey analysts—it's like "put some lipstick on," ya know? Sunflower seed?

VIRGINIA: What?

JIM: They don't let you smoke in these places and I have what the Freudians call an oral fixation.

(VIRGINIA *takes one.*)

VIRGINIA: Is this some kind of sabotage, you giving me something that'll be stuck in my teeth?

JIM: I would never sabotage you, Ginnie.

VIRGINIA: That's only because we're not on the same show.

JIM: No. It's because we're on the same side.

VOICE: Ms Eames? Stand by.

VIRGINIA: What am I supposed to do with the shell?

(JIM *puts his hand in front of* VIRGINIA'*s mouth.*)

JIM: Here.

VIRGINIA: I'm not going to spit in your hand.

JIM: Do it.

(VIRGINIA *spits the shell into* JIM'*s hand and winces.*)

VIRGINIA: What, are you, my dad?

(JIM *grins.*)

JIM: It helps to count off. You know, five, four, three with the red light flashing.
(*He backs up and watches her.*)

VIRGINIA: Five, four, three—
(*She silently thinks "2" and on "1" She smiles brilliantly into the camera.*)
Thank you for having me.

Scene Six
Lowering standards:
Virginia addresses the woman problem.

(VIRGINIA *on video, very polished. Title under her face:*
Virginia Eames, Commentary)

VIRGINIA: What is it with feminists these days?

In the Abu Ghraib trials, everyone is looking to blame the Bush administration for how such abominations could have occurred. And yet, liberals are uninterested in one vital fact: seven people were court-martialed in Abu Ghraib. Three of them were women.

Now, ladies, I know we're not so good with our mathematical skills but let me throw some statistics at you. Women only make up fifteen percent of the military force and yet, we make up forty-five percent of the Abu Ghraib criminals.

Why do you think that is? Feminists would like to say that discrimination leads women to "act out" in this way without mentioning that to allow women, the military has had to *lower* its standards.

Even on American soil, in a study of public safety officers, those of the female persuasion were found to have up to fifty-six percent less upper body strength. These Police-woman Barbies were also found to have thirty to forty percent less lower body strength than male officers. They were also a hundred percent more likely to feel "not fresh" during that time of the month.

When are we going to stop catering to feminists and their need for watered down standards? I mean, they fight for women to serve in the military and we have to save Jessica Lynch because her heel broke and Private Lynndie is sending us "thumbs up—wish you were here" postcards from Iraq.

Women have to admit there are some things we're just not good at—policework, the military and parallel parking.

Scene Seven
Tell me what you see:
Daniel gives Virginia some advice.

(VIRGINIA *and* DANIEL *on a couch in her apartment. They are watching a video of her performance.*)

DANIEL: What are we watching?

VIRGINIA: Me on Fox, yesterday.

DANIEL: And what are we looking for?

VIRGINIA: Ways to make me better.

DANIEL: Turning down the volume helps.

(VIRGINIA *hits* DANIEL *in the arm.*)

DANIEL: Ow!

VIRGINIA: I've got this thing tomorrow. I'm freaking out about it.

DANIEL: I figured.

VIRGINIA: Why?

DANIEL: Well, that's when you call. When you need an ego boost.

VIRGINIA: Daniel, that's not true.

(DANIEL *watches the T V.* VIRGINIA *looks at him.*)

VIRGINIA: Is it?

DANIEL: "People say."

VIRGINIA: What.

DANIEL: *(Referring to the T V)* You use that a lot, instead of a source. "People say that social security is in crisis." "Critics say."

VIRGINIA: Jim told me to.

DANIEL: Ah.

VIRGINIA: It's not a newspaper, Daniel.

DANIEL: You should be glad it's not.

VIRGINIA: Why?

DANIEL: Because then you'd have to run retractions when you get the facts wrong.

VIRGINIA: It's opinion journalism.

DANIEL: Different form.

VIRGINIA: Yes.

DANIEL: Mutant entity.

VIRGINIA: Daniel.

DANIEL: *(Again referring to the T V)* Then you should say, "I think" when you're stating your opinion.

VIRGINIA: Jim told me not to.

DANIEL: Oh.

VIRGINIA: Makes me look weak.

DANIEL: Why am I here again?

(VIRGINIA looks at DANIEL.)

DANIEL: Because you're "freaking out", right.

(VIRGINIA turns off the T V. DANIEL gets up, pours himself a drink.)

DANIEL: I remember when Jim trained politicians, not pundits. For some reason, that seemed like a nobler cause. Same thing, I guess.

VIRGINIA: Did you know him well, back in the day?

DANIEL: I went to his daughter's funeral.

VIRGINIA: Jim had a daughter?

DANIEL: Yeah. She was hit by a drunk driver, God, long time ago. Back when we were working on the McGovern campaign.

VIRGINIA: Jim worked for McGovern?

DANIEL: What do you two *talk* about?

VIRGINIA: We talk about me. I can't believe Jim worked for McGovern.

DANIEL: Yeah, Jim puts the "neo" in "Neo-con".

VIRGINIA: So is that what you have against him? He betrayed your ideals?

DANIEL: Um, no. He betrayed his own ideals.

VIRGINIA: What about me?

DANIEL: What about you?

(VIRGINIA *takes a sip from* DANIEL's *drink.*)

VIRGINIA: Am I betraying my ideals.

DANIEL: I'm not sure you have any.

VIRGINIA: *(Not particularly upset)* That's not a very nice thing to say.

DANIEL: What do you want me to say? "Virginia, I really love it when you say that Democrats are racist traitors"? Well, I don't.

VIRGINIA: I'm doing my job.

DANIEL: But you don't really believe it, you're just trying to be shocking.

VIRGINIA: Daniel, there are people who do believe these things. In fact, there are a *lot* of people who believe these things and they don't have a voice.

DANIEL: Ah, so, you're speaking on behalf of the "silent majority."

VIRGINIA: Someone needs to.

DANIEL: Why does it have to be you?

VIRGINIA: I'm not afraid to say the things that people think but won't say.

DANIEL: But civilization is built on people suppressing their base, angry impulses so that we can live together in some sort of peace.

VIRGINIA: *(Teasing)* I love it when you get didactic.

DANIEL: Look, all I'm saying is that's why we have reason and intellect.

VIRGINIA: And why is that?

DANIEL: So that we don't just say every awful thought that comes to mind.

(VIRGINIA stretches out on the couch. DANIEL stands, his drink in hand looking at her.)

VIRGINIA: It's got a basic draw, though, you have to admit.

DANIEL: What?

VIRGINIA: Something that you're not supposed to say. Or do.
It has a pull.

DANIEL: Yes. It has a pull.

VIRGINIA: *(Disarming)* I just talk on T V, Daniel. I'm not burning crosses in Barak Obama's backyard.

DANIEL: But you don't believe everything you say.

VIRGINIA: What if I believed it?

DANIEL: But you don't.

VIRGINIA: But what if I did.

DANIEL: But you don't.
(He sits down on the couch next to her.)
Or else we wouldn't be friends.

VIRGINIA: You'd stop being friends with me?

DANIEL: We were talking about your opinions. And how they affect our friendship.

VIRGINIA: We're more than friends, Daniel.

DANIEL: Are we?

VIRGINIA: Of course we are.
(She touches him.)

DANIEL: Um.

VIRGINIA: What?

DANIEL: I think this is the part where you sleep with me again to, you know, feel confident about yourself. And if I were younger, I'd jump at the chance. But I'm not. Younger.

VIRGINIA: No. You're not.

DANIEL: I should go—I'm not sure what I was thinking. Bad idea.

VIRGINIA: Do *you* think that it's a bad idea?

DANIEL: "People say" this is a bad idea.

VIRGINIA: You're learning.
(Pause)
Stay. Help me with this piece tomorrow. Friends, you know?

(DANIEL is thinking.)

VIRGINIA: You just made yourself a drink. Don't let good Scotch go to waste.
(She turns the monitor to him and sits in front of her videocamera. The shot is from the hip up.)
I need you. Be Jim. Tell me what I'm doing wrong.

DANIEL: Oh, God, where do I start.

(VIRGINIA throws a pillow at DANIEL.)

DANIEL: Okay, you—

VIRGINIA: Don't look at me.

DANIEL: What?

VIRGINIA: Look at the monitor. Tell me what you see.

(DANIEL *looks at the monitor, analyzing.*)

DANIEL: You tend to—

VIRGINIA: What—

DANIEL: You tend to lean forward, when you're making a point. I'm no expert—but it makes you look— Needy, I guess.

(VIRGINIA *makes a face and leans back.*)

DANIEL: You're very reactive.

VIRGINIA: What do you mean?

DANIEL: When someone says something you don't like, I see it. On your face.

VIRGINIA: And that's bad.

DANIEL: I like it. I can always see when you've come up with a joke. Your eyebrows lift up and I know a punchline's coming. I don't know what Jim thinks...

VIRGINIA: Jim likes it.

DANIEL: Good for him.

You crook your head.

VIRGINIA: What?

DANIEL: Put your head down—

(DANIEL *tries to gesture with his head that* VIRGINIA *should lower her chin. She's uncertain.*)

VIRGINIA: Like...?

(DANIEL *walks up to* VIRGINIA. *Looking at her image in the monitor, he moves her head with his hand.*)

DANIEL: A direct gaze—

(VIRGINIA *looks deeply into the camera, challenging* DANIEL. *He moves his hand on her face, stroking her cheek.*)

DANIEL: Um.

(VIRGINIA closes her eyes. DANIEL's eyes never leave the screen as his hand moves down her neck, to her chest.)

DANIEL: Jesus.

(DANIEL walks around to the side of VIRGINIA, still looking at the monitor. Kneeling next to her, he puts his hand on her thigh. He watches her face on the monitor as he moves his hand between her legs. She begins to breathe faster.)

(DANIEL's cell phone begins to ring.)

VIRGINIA: *(Her eyes still closed)* Don't pick it up.

DANIEL: You know I have to.
(For a beat, he stands, his head in his hand. He looks at the phone.)
It's Pat.
(Answering the phone) Yes? I'll be there soon.
(He walks over to the T V, turns on the news.)
Jeffrey Roth's been beheaded.

(DANIEL and VIRGINIA watch the T V, both horrified.)

VIRGINIA: I think I'm going to be sick.

DANIEL: He has a wife and a child.

VIRGINIA: This is what we're up against, Daniel.

DANIEL: Don't.

VIRGINIA: What?

DANIEL: Can we change the station, see if someone else has more information.

(VIRGINIA changes the channel. DANIEL and VIRGINIA watch for a beat.)

VIRGINIA: It's like if you watch it, you can control it.

DANIEL: Same images, different running text. They don't say who it was.

VIRGINIA: It doesn't matter anymore.

DANIEL: Of course it does.

VIRGINIA: Same result. Another dead American.

DANIEL: Their nationality matters, their cause matters.

VIRGINIA: What, so the A C L U can defend their *rights*?

DANIEL: Please shut up.

(VIRGINIA *takes the remote from* DANIEL *and turns off the T V.*)

VIRGINIA: Can you be on our side for one fucking moment!?

DANIEL: I am on "our side". I just think we need to be INFORMED.

VIRGINIA: We are informed. How much more information do you need?

DANIEL: Other countries live with this, they live with these images, this instability every day.

VIRGINIA: Am I wrong not to want to?
I don't *want* to know what it's like to live in the Middle East! If I wanted to know what it was like, I would live there. But I live *here*.

DANIEL: That won't keep you safe, not anymore.

VIRGINIA: That's what I'm saying! And you still want to sit around and wait for the *facts* to come in—

DANIEL: That's my job! Believe it or not, facts count for something. It's not just spin or how you phrase things—

VIRGINIA: What would it take? Would it have to be *me* there, some Arab's knife at my neck?

DANIEL: Stop it.

VIRGINIA: Would that make it real to you or would you just sit back / and watch?

(DANIEL *gets up to get his coat.* VIRGINIA *follows him.*)

DANIEL: *(Low)* God, what was / I *thinking*?

VIRGINIA: *(Overlapping)* You wouldn't protect me, would you, if it were me. If you had the chance, you would watch them kill me rather than actually DO something!

(DANIEL turns on VIRGINIA.)

DANIEL: You think you're worth dying for? You're not.

VIRGINIA: Well, that just sums / you guys up—

DANIEL: I can't *believe* / you—

VIRGINIA: What is worth dying for, / Daniel? Tell me that.

DANIEL: How can you be worth dying for when I can't even *listen* to you?

VIRGINIA: I don't need you to listen to me anymore—I have an audience, I have people who want to hear what I have / to say.

DANIEL: Nobody's listening / to you.

VIRGINIA: They are!

DANIEL: They just like looking at you. They just want to fuck you.

VIRGINIA: That's not true.

DANIEL: Why not? That's all I want.

(There's a moment where VIRGINIA looks like she's been punched in the stomach.)

DANIEL: Virginia—I wanted to hurt you and so I did.

(DANIEL goes to VIRGINIA, she moves away from him.)

DANIEL: Let's rewind. I was helping you, you needed me.

(VIRGINIA looks at DANIEL for a beat.)

VIRGINIA: You want to help, let me try some new material on you.

DANIEL: Uh, / sure.

VIRGINIA: A policeman walks up to a man who's just poured gasoline on a Muslim / and set him on fire—

DANIEL: Virginia—

VIRGINIA: And the policeman says, what are you doing?

DANIEL: Don't.

VIRGINIA: And the man says, "Oh, about three to a gallon".

(She resets her video camera to a close-up, ignoring him.)

Now get the fuck out of my apartment. I have a show to prepare.

(VIRGINIA sits in front of her camera. DANIEL leaves. She levels her eyes into the camera.)

VIRGINIA: We don't truly understand what we want. From our country, from our politicians, from ourselves. We look to others for answers.
We look to others *not only* for answers but we allow other countries to define our perception of ourselves. Vietnam says we are guilty, therefore we are guilty. Iraq says we are guilty, therefore we are guilty. Governments that are not even governments accuse us of their worst crimes. Who's next, who else will find us accountable? And of what?
What's worse is that WE believe it. These ideas become a part of us…
No longer a list of accomplishments, American history has become a list of transgressions.
(She is aggressively trying not to cry.)
History belongs to those who write it. Why do we choose to write a history to feel ashamed of?
I'm not ashamed.
Fuck.

(She cries.)
(Her face changes, she gets a driven look.)
(She slaps her own face. Hard)
(It wasn't enough.)
(She slaps it again.)
(She looks at the camera again, her cheek reddening. There are no remnants of her tears from a few moments before. She looks into the camera, defined.)
I am not ashamed.

END OF ACT ONE

ACT TWO

Scene Eight
Extolling the virtues:
Virginia and Irene discuss the war.

*(The Press Speaks studio, in the middle of the show.
Aggressive)*

IRENE: You've been saying—

VIRGINIA: Yes?

IRENE: Some inflammatory things—

VIRGINIA: I've gotten a lot of support so I don't know
how inflammatory—

IRENE: —on your blog about how the press is handling
the war.

VIRGINIA: Mishandling? Yes.

IRENE: Do you think it might be handled better?

VIRGINIA: Obviously. One of my many complaints is
the persistent comparison to Vietnam—

IRENE: It's a relevant metaphor—

VIRGINIA: How?

IRENE: What?

VIRGINIA: How is it a relevant metaphor? How is a war
that was engaged *(by a democratic president, mind you)*
in South East Asia to fend off *communism* anything like

a war in the Middle East that began ten years ago as a
result of *Iraq's* invasion of a smaller country?

IRENE: In that it's a war that the American people
didn't want.

VIRGINIA: So in other words, all wars are the same.
In the beginning, World War II was a war that the
American people didn't want either. Would *you* like to
live under the rule of Saddam Hussein?

IRENE: Of course not.

VIRGINIA: After your show last week, listing the
positive attributes of Iraq's secular nation under
Saddam, I wasn't sure *what* to think.

IRENE: I was *trying* to differentiate between Al Qaeda's
Islamic fundamentalism and the Iraqi people's
beliefs—

VIRGINIA: Do you think the American people are
stupid?

IRENE: No, but more than twenty percent of Americans
mistakenly believe that Iraq helped plan 9/11.

VIRGINIA: Well, we don't actually know, do we?

IRENE: Actually, we do. The 9/11 commission found no
credible / evidence—

VIRGINIA: I'm just saying, your choice of topic suggests
that you think Americans don't follow the news, that
they can't make up their own minds.

IRENE: It's my job to present the news in a way that
people understand.

VIRGINIA: I trust the American people to "differentiate"
between black and white.

IRENE: Is that why you called me the—
(Looks at a piece of paper)
"Leni Riefenstahl of the liberal left?"

VIRGINIA: Try saying *that* three times fast.

IRENE: Comparing me to Hitler's propagandist is a *joke* to you?

VIRGINIA: *(Unfazed)* Some film critics think her 1938 film "Olympia" is one of the only masterpieces filmed by a woman.

IRENE: I should be *flattered*?

VIRGINIA: You should take compliments when they come.

IRENE: I object to being attacked when I'm doing my job.

VIRGINIA: A lot of people are just doing their job. I'm sure Iraqi homicide bombers feel the same way on a bad day.

IRENE: I'm reporting news and you're accusing me of some kind of *bias*. Not only liberal bias but *anti-American* bias.

VIRGINIA: That piece wasn't supposed to change people's minds?

IRENE: That piece was supposed to make people think. It was supposed to give my viewers additional information that perhaps has been left behind in the *rhetoric*.

VIRGINIA: Saddam controlled their newspaper, their T V. He told them what to think for years. What *we're* trying to do is to allow the Iraqi people to have their own ideas.

IRENE: It might be difficult for us to export a free press when we're paying Iraqi newspapers to run articles written by *our* military.

VIRGINIA: I just want the American people to know how much they are manipulated by what the media / chooses to present—

IRENE: Oh, let's not get into the "liberal media"—

VIRGINIA: When we were invading Afghanistan, it was great to talk about the oppression of women but when it came to Iraq, the liberal media kept its mouth shut.

IRENE: Iraq had a secular government—

VIRGINIA: Right, and in 1999, Saddam's brother beheaded fifty / women—

IRENE: Ms Eames—

VIRGINIA: —and their heads were nailed to the doors of their houses and left to hang for days—that's not exactly women's lib.

IRENE: And I'm not defending that, I'm—

VIRGINIA: Where was your National Organization for Women? More importantly, where was Susan Sarandon?

IRENE: Since the interim government has been installed, Iraqi women have been attacked in the streets for not wearing burkas. So let's not pretend that the American government was fighting for women's rights / in Iraq.

VIRGINIA: *(Changing the subject)* Last month, we saw Jeffery Roth beheaded. That / may be a normal day in Iraq, but I don't want it to be a normal occurrence in America. Do you?

IRENE: You're changing the subject, Ms Eames, You're changing the *subject*—

VIRGINIA: No, I'm not, I'm saying that you should think twice before you create pieces extolling the virtues of Iraqi daily life. You have a responsibility, Irene.

(IRENE *looks away from* VIRGINIA *into the camera.*)

IRENE: We're out of time. I appreciate your coming on the show, Ms Eames.

VIRGINIA: It's always a pleasure, Ms Shay.

IRENE: And now we go to Ben in the Sudan.

(Music plays. IRENE *takes off her microphone, furious.* VIRGINIA *is energized, as if she just played a great game of tennis.)*

VIRGINIA: Thank you for asking me on the show, Irene. I was glad to have the opportunity to defend my column.

IRENE: *(Flatly)* You're welcome.

VIRGINIA: No, I mean it, it's rare that a conservative viewpoint is given airtime in this climate.

IRENE: I do try to have balanced show, Virginia.

*(*VIRGINIA *starts to leave. She stops and turns.)*

VIRGINIA: Oh, Irene. Jim Lauderdale says hello.

Scene Nine
Cat Fights:
Pat drinks to Virginia's success.

*(*VIRGINIA *and* PAT *on the couch in* VIRGINIA*'s apartment. A bottle of wine between them. They're a little sloppy.)*

PAT: To the lowest common denominator.

VIRGINIA: Oh come on.

PAT: To cat fights.

VIRGINIA: *(A good sport)* I'll drink to that.

*(*PAT *and* VIRGINIA *clink their glasses.)*

PAT: What is it, do you think?

VIRGINIA: What.

PAT: The whole cat fight thing. You're on with men all the time but all people can talk about is the Irene and Virginia celebrity death match.

VIRGINIA: Voyeurism.

PAT: What, they want to see the good girl with her teeth bared?

VIRGINIA: Pat, don't be so naïve, they're hoping that once we climb into the mudpit and get really vicious, we might just start kissing.

PAT: And they get to watch.

VIRGINIA: It is for them after all.

PAT: An evening's entertainment.

VIRGINIA: Speaking of an evening's entertainment— *(She dumps a bag of letters on the coffee table.)*

PAT: What, my dear, is this? Fan mail?

VIRGINIA: Polar opposite.

PAT: This is hate mail?

VIRGINIA: Yep. The people who love me post to my website. The people who hate me are Luddites.

PAT: *(In admiring awe)* Virginia, you—are—hated.

VIRGINIA: *(With a happy grin)* I *know!*
Let's sort them into categories.
"You're a liar."
"You're dumb."
And "I hate you for miscellaneous reasons."

(PAT and VIRGINIA start to sort.)

PAT: I've never gotten hate mail. The paper does.

VIRGINIA: The people have spoken.

PAT: *(Looking at a letter)* This is a very long one saying you're dumb. Oh, look, it's got footnotes.
(She places it in the dumb pile.)
What's crazy is that it's actually changing what we write. I mean, we got a memo from the conglomerate upstairs that we couldn't include the number of

American soldiers dead in articles that weren't specifically about casualities. That *that* showed bias.

VIRGINIA: Why do people have such bad handwriting? I can't read the insults. Does that say "limbo"?

*(*PAT *and* VIRGINIA *look at each other.)*

VIRGINIA: Oh, "Bimbo". Of course.

PAT: When including *facts* in an article about the war is considered bias, we're in a bad way.

VIRGINIA: You'll love this one.

*(*VIRGINIA *passes* PAT *a letter.)*

PAT: "You are so full of shit. Your piece—"
Wait a minute. "Piece" is spelled wrong, "I" before "E", motherfucker.
(She corrects the letter with a pen.)

VIRGINIA: You're supposed to read the hate mail, not edit it.

PAT: "Your piece on Clinton's early scandals in Arkansas, Troopergate, neglects to mention that each of the state troopers were paid thousands of dollars for their stories."

VIRGINIA: Seven years later, Bill's still getting blowjobs while he's on the phone with Castro.

PAT: At least he was multi-tasking.

VIRGINIA: *(Referring to the joke)* Can I use that?

PAT: "You misquote the date of the Paula Jones trial."
Well, he's got a point there.

VIRGINIA: He's just mad that I'm right about the important things.

PAT: But Virginia, you did get the date wrong. I'm surprised your fact-checkers didn't catch it.

VIRGINIA: *(Ignoring her)* Let me find a better one.

PAT: You do have a fact-checker, don't you?

VIRGINIA: "You're an asshole." Short and sweet. Miscellaneous.

PAT: You have fact-checkers, right?

VIRGINIA: It's a website. They don't have the money.

PAT: You're funded by pharmaceutical companies and oil men, how can you not have the money?

VIRGINIA: Pat, we were having a good time, don't ruin it by getting all liberal on me.

PAT: I don't think it's *liberal* to want you to get your facts right—

VIRGINIA: "I saw you on that show, the one with the old senator."
Uuh, you'll have to be more specific...
"Do you think—"

PAT: *(Another letter)* "I'd like to see *you* in a war zone, crying and helpless. I'd like to see you with your legs cut off because of the gangrene."

VIRGINIA: It's always about my legs. Who knew Democrats were such leg men?

PAT: "I'll see you in hell, you nazi bitch."

VIRGINIA: *(Unaffected)* That one isn't that funny, let me—

PAT: You should report this to the police, Virginia.

VIRGINIA: I don't bother.

PAT: It's a threat.

VIRGINIA: What, he's going to give me *gangrene*?

PAT: It's terrifying.

VIRGINIA: It's nothing personal.

PAT: How can it not be personal?

VIRGINIA: Pat, you have to keep in mind, these letters are coming from the most passive, repressed political party in the history of man, oh, I'm sorry, in the history of *woman*, because they're all neutered idiots.

PAT: A) I *am* a woman and B) I'm not an idiot.

VIRGINIA: I wasn't talking about you.

PAT: Yes, you were.

VIRGINIA: I'm just saying, I'm not scared of liberal men attacking me physically. If they don't want to attack terrorists, they're not going to attack me. Besides, that's what being right does to you. It liberates you from fear.

PAT: I'm not a guest on one of your shows. Don't rant at me.

VIRGINIA: I'm not ranting.

PAT: Yes, you are. I used to like talking to you, in fact, I used to enjoy *arguing* with you and now—

VIRGINIA: What?

PAT: And now, I don't know who I'm arguing with. Is this Jim Lauderdale? Is it Bush? Who exactly is in there?

VIRGINIA: This is me.

PAT: But everything you say is on a loop. According to you, Clinton couldn't do one thing right and Bush is blameless.

VIRGINIA: What about you? I mean, *you* name one thing that Bush has done right. Go.

(PAT *thinks for a second.*)

PAT: *(Defiantly)* I can't.

VIRGINIA: No, you *won't*. You get so blind when you talk about Bush, you can't see straight. I mean, Muslim terrorists, we have to try to understand them, we have to give *them* the benefit of the doubt but Bush, him you hate.

PAT: Bush *works* for me! I have no control over Al Qaeda; they're not doing a job I PAY them for!

VIRGINIA: But you didn't hire him. The rest of America did!

PAT: The rest of America? Fifty-two percent is not a *mandate!*

VIRGINIA: We. Still. Won.

(PAT *declines to comment. She goes back to the letters.*)

PAT: I still think you should report the "nazi bitch" letter.

VIRGINIA: I can handle it.

PAT: Does Daniel know you get all this hate mail?

VIRGINIA: Um. No. We haven't—

PAT: Oh, right, you had that falling out. He told me.

VIRGINIA: He did?

PAT: I'm sure it'll iron itself out. You two were so close.

VIRGINIA: Maybe.

PAT: At some point, the three of us will all be adults and meet for lunch. Maybe the four of us, you could bring some nice young man and we'll have brunch some Sunday. Melon and mimosas.

VIRGINIA: How is he?

PAT: I think he's really good. I think he's doing really well.
(She goes back to a letter.)
Recovering.

VIRGINIA: From what?

(PAT *makes a vague hand gesture.*)

PAT: Oh, you know. Everything. The newspaper business becoming virtually obsolete in our lifetime, that's not an easy adjustment.

VIRGINIA: I bet.

PAT: Virginia. I'm sure Daniel didn't tell you—even as close as you are—well, that things have…progressed since you left.

VIRGINIA: Progressed?

PAT: It's hard at this age to put a name on it, you know? What, we're dating? *(She laughs.)* Seeing each other? Those are words for much younger people. People like you. Are you seeing anybody?

VIRGINIA: No.

PAT: Too busy, I guess.

VIRGINIA: Yes. How long?

PAT: Hm?

VIRGINIA: You and Daniel, how long has it been.

PAT: Sometime after you quit *The Post*. Oh, wait a minute, you didn't quit, you were fired. But when you started doing your shows, when was that?

VIRGINIA: February.

PAT: Right. After that.

VIRGINIA: He didn't mention it.

PAT: He wouldn't. So secretive, that man.

VIRGINIA: Yes.

PAT: But we should do that—get things out in the open. Sometime after you and Daniel patch things up, we'll all go out, the three of us. Or the four of us. You and some age-appropriate man.

VIRGINIA: Yeah. Me and the appropriate man.

PAT: That would be nice. We should do that.

(She goes back to reading a letter.)
We really should.

(PAT continues to read the letter. VIRGINIA doesn't say anything.)

Scene Ten
A part of the world:
Suzanne Roth speaks in her husband's memory.

(On video: A Press Conference. SUZANNE speaks. Throughout the speech, there are shutters clicking and sporadic flashes. She isn't practiced, she has notes.)

SUZANNE: People have asked me how Jeffrey could've put his reporting first, before me and Sarah. But Jeffrey and I never saw it that way. We always felt that we were a part of the world, that it was his job to tell us what was going on, whether it was making us aware of what our troops are going through in Iraq or to let us know how bad the fighting is. His job was not to let us forget. And that's very easy.
It's very easy to forget here. Unless it affects you personally. And it has. Affected me.
I would like to thank the amazing people of America for all of your support and condolences. It's been— tremendous. The love that we've received from complete strangers has been astounding.
However, I would like to ask the politicians and commentators who are using my husband's name to stop unless, of course, you understand what my husband stood for.
My husband did not support the war in Iraq.
He did not support the Patriot Act.
He did not support what he felt were excessive detentions in Guantanamo Bay.

So I would ask, out of respect for my husband and his
views, that this exploitation end.
Thank you very much. No questions. Thank you.

Scene Eleven
A joke:
A Democrat and a Republican walk into a bar…

*(A smoky old man Irish bar. A T V over the bar shows the
baseball game. This is not a bar to pick up women, this is a
bar to talk.)*

*(*DANIEL *sits, drinking a scotch and soda. He has already
had one, not tight in any way, but had one for courage. He
watches the game and waits for* JIM, *who is five minutes
late. He looks at his watch and then decides that he should
go.* JIM *enters, sees* DANIEL. DANIEL *realizes he missed his
chance to leave and sits down, resigned.* JIM *is happy to see*
DANIEL.)*

JIM: Daniel.

DANIEL: Jim.

JIM: This was a surprise.

DANIEL: Was it?

JIM: Aw, come on, you old dog, I haven't seen you
since… when was it?

DANIEL: With Virginia, the studio—

JIM: Nah, "seen you" seen you. I mean, we see each
other all the time, in the hallways at school, if you
know what I'm saying. But sat down and *saw* each
other, it's been awhile.
(To the bartender) A Maker's Mark, neat, thanks.

DANIEL: Yes. It's been awhile.

JIM: *(A slight question)* So this is about Virginia.

(JIM *waits for affirmation.* DANIEL *is silent.*)

JIM: *(To the bartender)* Make it a double, it's gonna be a long night.
Well, how the hell are ya?

DANIEL: Managing.

JIM: Managing? That doesn't sound good, Dan.

DANIEL: How are *you*, Jim?

JIM: *(With appetite) Great.* Never been better.

DANIEL: Of course.

(DANIEL *laughs.* JIM *chuckles too.*)

DANIEL: Of course you are.

JIM: You think it's easy to be this chipper in the face of the apocalypse?

DANIEL: *(Smiling)* Certainly not.

JIM: It's hard, I'm telling you, it's a burden.

(DANIEL *and* JIM *sip.*)

DANIEL: So.

JIM: So.

DANIEL: Virginia's interview with the widow of Jeffery Roth.

JIM: Ah, yes.

DANIEL: She's not going to do it, is she?

JIM: How'd you hear about that?

DANIEL: I don't know, Jim. It might have been some "undisclosed source" that informed the media that Virginia is preparing to confront Suzanne Roth on the air. I think that might be where I heard it.

JIM: "I can neither confirm nor deny the rumors."

DANIEL: Give it a break, Jim.

JIM: Obviously, if Virginia wants to have a civil discussion with the bereaved spokeswoman of the radical left, that's up to her.

DANIEL: But it won't be civil. That's not what you do.

JIM: What's your interest in the situation? You're just Ginnie's ex-boss, right? I mean, I know you got that whole father/daughter dynamic and that's cute but she's a big girl now.

DANIEL: Look, Jim, Virginia means a lot to me.

JIM: If she means so much to you, you should've fought the newspaper when they fired her.

DANIEL: That was a complicated situation.

JIM: Way to watch your babygirl's back, Danny boy.

DANIEL: She was pushing to get fired. That's what she wanted; that's what she got.

JIM: She was just trying to get your attention.
(He looks away, up at a T V.)
God*damn*it, my team's doing poorly.

DANIEL: And who's your team this year, Jim?

JIM: It's who it always is. Anybody who's up / against the Yankees, that's who.

DANIEL: *(Remembering)* Against the Yankees, that's who. Right, I forgot about that…
How is she?

JIM: Virginia?

DANIEL: Yes.

JIM: On the mend.

DANIEL: From what?

JIM: Some guy.

DANIEL: There's a guy?

JIM: Was.

DANIEL: Was.

JIM: Maybe you know him, some guy at the paper.

DANIEL: I don't think I do.

JIM: Ah, too bad. If you knew who he was, I would tell you to take him out to the woodshed. It would be a nice paternal thing to do.

DANIEL: Sure.

JIM: I rib her about boys, you know, just to check on my investment, make sure she's not gonna give it all up and run off with some businessman or T V producer. She just smiles and drops the topic.
She goes home to her new sofa and coffee table, she can afford furniture now, and she watches her tapes, works on the next day's shows. A hard worker, our Virginia.

DANIEL: All the more reason not to let her go down in flames.

JIM: Publicity is carnivorous, it feeds on itself. Somethin's gotta keep the blood in the water.

DANIEL: Is that the world we're living in now?

JIM: I don't know, Daniel, what world are *you* living in?

DANIEL: You were always smart, Jim.

JIM: How's that?

DANIEL: You saw which way the wind was blowing, you shifted perspectives, you shifted careers.

JIM: My perspective was shifted by force.

DANIEL: I guess you'd see it that way.

JIM: Remember how right we were, so certain.

DANIEL: We were. We were right.

JIM: Sure, we were right until Saigon fell. Then the commissions, the atrocities, and best yet, reports that the Viet Cong kept fighting for years because they knew that the youth of America was marching on the streets against the war. We kept that war going for *years* with our protests. Remember that, Danny? College kids spitting on the American soldiers who came back? I don't look back with pride on the sixties, I look back and I'm damn near ashamed.

DANIEL: I'm not.

JIM: We just learned different things, Dan.

DANIEL: I learned that we make mistakes and we have to atone for them.

JIM: *(Amused)* "Atone"? Listen to you! That's the thing about you guys. So masochistic. It's like you wanna punish yourselves for being successful, flagellate yourselves for being number one.

DANIEL: What, being "number one" is our right?

JIM: No, it's our privilege. One we take seriously.

DANIEL: Virginia has that same certainty. It must be nice not to question…everything.

JIM: It is. It is nice.

(DANIEL and JIM sip.)

DANIEL: Tell Virginia not to do the show with Suzanne Roth.

JIM: And why not, Daniel?

DANIEL: I don't want her pathology to be aired for everyone to see, that's why.

JIM: What you call pathology, some people call opinions. Being a Republican ain't a disease, Daniel.

DANIEL: I don't even know why I'm talking to you about it. I'll just call her myself and tell her what I think.

JIM: Fine, call her. Do me a favor.

DANIEL: What?

JIM: Make the call. Use my cell.

(JIM *throws his phone down on the bar*. DANIEL *looks at it, figures something out.*)

DANIEL: She doesn't want to do it, does she?

JIM: *(Annoyed)* She'll do it.

DANIEL: *(A smile)* She's fighting you on it. She's digging her heels in.

JIM: And what makes you think that?

DANIEL: *That's* why you released the story to the media, to pressure her. And maybe that's why you came when I called—so you could somehow use me to stir up one of her adolescent rebellions.
(He is really tickled by this.)
The puppetmaster has dropped the strings! You thought she'd just do your bidding but she's a little more complicated than that.
Well, good for her.
(He's a little impressed, a little wistful. Perhaps he gives a small toast to Virginia before he drinks.)

JIM: You don't have to be so smug about it.

(DANIEL *claps* JIM *on the back.*)

DANIEL: Don't feel bad, Jimbo, we all lose our mojo at some point.

JIM: *(Casually)* I knew you wouldn't call her, Danny.

DANIEL: And how did you figure that out, maestro?

JIM: Daniel, three times, I've called Virginia your daughter, made jokes about you being her dad. Not once did you correct me and say, "No, she was my girlfriend. We loved each other."

(DANIEL *stops smiling.*)

JIM: No wonder she pulled that "Bush pin" crap. Maybe she was sick of being your dirty secret.

DANIEL: She wasn't—

JIM: It's fun having a dirty secret, believe me I know, but it's not fun being one.

DANIEL: I don't need you to lecture me, thanks.

JIM: No, you got that going on in your head all the time, dontchya, sport?

(DANIEL *gets up, pulls a twenty out of his wallet.*)

DANIEL: *(Tautly)* Buy your drink out of this. I'm going.

JIM: Naw, I got it.

DANIEL: I asked you here.

JIM: I pay my own way, Danny.

DANIEL: No. Put your money back in your goddamned pocket, Jim.
You think you can *judge* me? Are you *kidding*? When you're using Virginia's compulsion or her low self esteem or her father issues to make yourself some *money*?

JIM: That's not all it is.

DANIEL: *(With a scornful laugh)* Oh right, you're affecting *change*.
(A shift into ferocity)
Look at what you do for a living, Jim.
In a magic act, the magician has two things going on at all times. One hand actually pulls the rabbit out of the hat, the other misdirects the eye.

And all this shit you're doing with Virginia, it's all misdirection. It's just smoke and mirrors. This way, everyone's yelling at Virginia, yelling at the T V, they're not actually dealing with the people in charge. So don't act like you have a higher calling. You're not even pulling the rabbit out of the hat.

JIM: And you think you're any different?

DANIEL: No. I know I'm not.

(JIM *puts his hands up, "you win".)*

JIM: Well, thanks. I never say no to a free drink.

(DANIEL *begins to leave.)*

JIM: Hey, Daniel. This was good. Old times.

(DANIEL *exits.* JIM *sips his drink.)*

Scene Twelve
Crossing over:
Jim tries to reason with Virginia.

(In the satellite studio. VIRGINIA *on a phone call, with cellular head gear.* JIM *working on his palm pilot.)*

VIRGINIA: Well, all I know is I'd like to see Ted Kennedy in a burka. Yeah. 'Cause he looks like an oompa-loompa.
(She gestures to JIM, *a yapping gesture with her hand, rolls her eyes.)*
Yeah. Suzanne Roth, yes, sure, she's grieving. But should we change policy because a woman lost her husband? There are a lot of soldiers' wives that could speak more effectively to her grief.
(She looks at her watch.)
I'm not going to answer that. I think you've gotten your half hour. Yes, well, thank you for having me. Thank you.

(She hangs up, throws the head gear across the room.)
If I talk to one more dinky morning radio show, I'm
going to go crazy.

JIM: That's why you have to host Irene's show—

VIRGINIA: Absolutely not.

JIM: It's national.

VIRGINIA: What's Sean Hannity doing this week? Is Bill
O'Reilly too busy sexually harassing his employees to
interview the grieving widow?

JIM: They have their own shows.

VIRGINIA: Right. Because they're men.

JIM: It's way too early in your career to play the gender
card, Ginnie.

VIRGINIA: So you think I should work my way up like
they did in the ol' days? Do talk radio for ten years?

JIM: Darlin' you'd be wasted on radio. No, they got
shows because they proved that they could carry a
show.

VIRGINIA: I can carry a show.

JIM: And here's the perfect opportunity to prove that,
by sitting in for Irene while she's on assignment. You
do it, you get taken seriously by a larger audience,
not just a conservative one. And all you have to do is
interview Suzanne Roth.

VIRGINIA: I told you I didn't want to do that.

JIM: The widow asked for you.

VIRGINIA: Right. Because she wants to lay into me on
national T V.

JIM: And so what if she does? You can handle her.

VIRGINIA: I don't know if I can.

JIM: A man can't take her on. If she doesn't talk to you, she'll do some fluff piece with Oprah in two months, everyone will wipe their eyes and say, "Why *don't* we pull out of Iraq? Aw hell, let's go easy on Iran, too." You got to scare her from getting back in the ring.

VIRGINIA: The world hates me enough as it is.

JIM: If the world hates you already, what do you got to lose?

VIRGINIA: Jim, I said no.

JIM: Okay, okay...

(There's a frustrated pause for both JIM *and* VIRGINIA. JIM *picks up a remote, turns up the piped-in music on the speaker.)*

VIRGINIA: What is this Muzak crap?

JIM: This isn't crap, darlin' it's a classic.

*(*JIM *turns it up a little, maybe* My Girl *by Otis Redding is playing.)*

VIRGINIA: How old are you anyway?

JIM: Let's just say, I got suits older than you.

VIRGINIA: You might wanna think about buying new ones.

JIM: I hear you like older men.

VIRGINIA: Older men like *me*.

*(*JIM *takes* VIRGINIA's *hand and begins dancing with her.)*

JIM: I saw Otis Redding at Monterey. A lotta people say they saw Otis at Monterey but I really did.

VIRGINIA: What were the old days like, Pops?

JIM: What people never realize about soul, real soul, is that it meant as much to us white hicks as it did to those black kids in the cities. More even.
Twenty-six years old, he died in a plane crash.

VIRGINIA: What is it with musicians and plane crashes.

JIM: They gotta get to their gigs. Stax records, the dream of crossing over, died with him.

VIRGINIA: If he crossed over, everyone would write about how he sold out his roots.

JIM: *Dock of the Bay*, it doesn't end with his usual adlibbing, you know, like gospel. It ends with him whistling like a country song. I never heard that as selling out, I heard it as reaching out.

(JIM and VIRGINIA stop dancing. He turns off the music.)

JIM: Everyone's dead, Virginia. All the great men. It's all bureaucrats and analysts, bunglers and amateurs. Lord save me from amateurs.

VIRGINIA: Is that what Suzanne Roth is?

JIM: 'Course. Gummi bear?

VIRGINIA: Camera adds ten pounds.

JIM: That's something you do not have to worry about.

(VIRGINIA still passes on the gummi bear.)

JIM: Doesn't anyone EAT anymore?
(He eats one.)
My kid used to love these. I had to buy 'em in a special candy store. They were only made in Switzerland then.

VIRGINIA: What was her name?

(JIM looks at VIRGINIA, surprised.)

JIM: Cadence.
(He looks back at his gummi bears.)
Life seems real simple when you lose someone to chaos. I know that better than anyone.
It isn't. Everything's causal. A drunk behind the wheel, but someone built that car, someone paved that road. And someone wasn't watching as carefully as he should've. You can lose someone in an instant.

To blame a war because you lost someone you loved, that's like blaming progress, blaming the invention of the steam engine.

(VIRGINIA *takes a gummi bear.*)

VIRGINIA: So. How do I win it—if I were to go on with Suzanne? How would I win an argument with the beloved widow?

JIM: They always say search for your opponent's weak spot, his Achilles heel. If Karl Rove has taught us anything, it is that you attack strengths. Strengths are the places where your opponents are unguarded, where they feel safe.

VIRGINIA: Yeah but—

JIM: No "buts." You're the only one who can do this.

VIRGINIA: If I do this, there's no going back.

JIM: Is that what you're scared of? That's the whole point! It's time to cross over, Virginia.

VIRGINIA: Fine, I'll do it.

JIM: Atta girl.

(JIM *lobs a jewelry box at* VIRGINIA.)

VIRGINIA: Is this some kind of payment?

JIM: It's nothin' special. We just gotta spruce up that black dress you're gonna wear.

(VIRGINIA *opens the box.*)

VIRGINIA: It's a cross.

JIM: Yeah.

VIRGINIA: It's very beautiful.

(JIM *approaches and takes the necklace from* VIRGINIA. *He puts it on her neck.*)

JIM: Filigree. I bought it in Italy.

VIRGINIA: When were you in Italy?

JIM: 1964.

VIRGINIA: Did you buy it for your daughter?

JIM: Yes.

VIRGINIA: —I can't—

JIM: Someone should wear it.
(He finishes. He walks back around, surveying her.)
There. Now you look the part.

Scene Thirteen
The Same Frame:
Virginia Eames defends her position to Suzanne Roth.

(IRENE and SUZANNE enter the T V studio. SUZANNE is understandably very nervous.)

IRENE: And here we are. This is the studio. That's your chair, she'll sit there.

SUZANNE: Ms Shay?

IRENE: Irene, you can call me Irene.

(SUZANNE sits down. She looks around.)

SUZANNE: Oh, Irene. Where do I look? I don't know— I've never done this before.

IRENE: Just look at her as if you're talking to her.

SUZANNE: I *will* be talking to her.

IRENE: *(Pointing the cameras out)* What I mean is that there are three cameras, her camera, your camera and one from the front that puts you in the same frame.

SUZANNE: *(Looking at the middle camera)* The same frame.

IRENE: We account for the fact that you're talking to each other. So you don't have to worry about where to look.

SUZANNE: I just have to worry about everything else.

IRENE: Don't say that. I'm not worried. You're going to be great.

(She smiles at her.)

SUZANNE: If you say so.

(VIRGINIA enters, and stops short when she sees IRENE. VIRGINIA is wearing a completely inappropriate little black dress.)

VIRGINIA: Irene.

IRENE: Virginia. Nice dress.

VIRGINIA: I thought you were out of town.

IRENE: Trip got cancelled.

VIRGINIA: It's not too late, I'll be glad to give you my seat and go and get a latte.

(IRENE and VIRGINIA both laugh falsely.)

VIRGINIA: You must be Suzanne. Virginia Eames.

(VIRGINIA extends her hand. SUZANNE pauses for a second before she takes it.)

SUZANNE: I know.

VIRGINIA: It's good to meet you.

IRENE: I'll be watching from the control room.

VIRGINIA: Well. Enjoy the show.

IRENE: *(To SUZANNE)* I'll see you afterwards.

SUZANNE: Thank you, Irene.

(There is an uncomfortable beat as VIRGINIA puts on her mike. She is searching for how to handle a difficult situation.)

VIRGINIA: *(Truthfully)* I'm—I'm very sorry for your loss.

SUZANNE: Aren't you going to wait until the cameras are on to commiserate. As an American.

VIRGINIA: I will probably mention it on camera. Is that okay?

SUZANNE: It's your interview.

VIRGINIA: So have you been doing the rounds? A lot of interviews, must be exhausting.

SUZANNE: This is my only one. I requested you and they made it happen.

VIRGINIA: They did.

SUZANNE: I don't really have much interest in being on T V.

VIRGINIA: Well, I'm glad you could make it—I'm glad you chose me to talk to.

SUZANNE: I've been—

(Music starts.)

MALE VOICE: Standby.

VIRGINIA: We're about to start.

(Music swells and the lights brighten.)

VIRGINIA: *(To the center camera)* This is *The Press Speaks* and I'm Virginia Eames in for Irene Shay, who's on assignment. Today we have with us Suzanne Roth, the widow of *Newsweek* reporter Jeffery Roth. We all watched in horror as the story unfolded, first when her husband was kidnapped and then watched with sadness as we heard the news that her husband had died at the hands of—religious extremists.
(Turns to SUZANNE) First, I want to say how sorry I am that your husband was killed.

SUZANNE: Thank you.

VIRGINIA: And thank you very much for being with us today.

(SUZANNE *silently nods.*)

VIRGINIA: It was tragic. He was obviously a very brave man.

SUZANNE: Yes.

VIRGINIA: Can you take us through the last few months?

SUZANNE: Well, it's been hard. Um. My husband was an amazing man, and a great reporter who went after a story relentlessly and his work often put him in dangerous positions. But he felt that first hand information was crucial to good reporting. That facts were essential. That may be surprising to you—

VIRGINIA: It's not.

SUZANNE: *(Firmly)* It may be surprising to you because I feel that you've made it your job in the last month to use my husband's death, to politicize my husband's murder without any regard to what he would want—

VIRGINIA: I feel that someone needs to speak for him—

SUZANNE: That's *my* job—

VIRGINIA: Since he can longer speak for himself.

SUZANNE: What makes you think you can speak for my husband at all?

VIRGINIA: We were in the same line of work—

SUZANNE: You are not in the same / line of work—

VIRGINIA: We're both reporters.

SUZANNE: You are a *pundit*. You comment in pithy ways about the events of the day. He was on the front line, finding the stories you then talk about.

VIRGINIA: So it's a question of authenticity?

SUZANNE: What?

VIRGINIA: That's the way it is with you liberals—

SUZANNE: I don't consider myself a / liberal.

VIRGINIA: Liberals, perhaps because they feel guilty about their upper class, private school / backgrounds—

SUZANNE: I didn't / have—

VIRGINIA: —are obsessed with authenticity. "You can't know what it's like unless you've lived it." All this empathy.

SUZANNE: And what's wrong with that?

VIRGINIA: Do you have empathy for the men who beheaded your husband?

SUZANNE: I want them punished within the limits of the law—within the limits of the Geneva Convention. But can I understand when a person has lost everything of value, when their country has been / brutalized—

VIRGINIA: Do you think your husband's murderers will be caught if the U S government is not rigorous?

SUZANNE: I think you can be rigorous and still allow for complexity.

VIRGINIA: I don't agree.

SUZANNE: By not allowing for complexity, you don't allow room for doubt.

VIRGINIA: I have no doubts.

SUZANNE: *(Amazed)* How can you not have *doubt*? When people's lives are at stake?

VIRGINIA: Try it, it's easy. Vote Republican.

SUZANNE: What is that supposed to be, a joke?

VIRGINIA: *(Caught off guard)* No.

SUZANNE: *American* lives are at stake. The world's opinion of us has never been lower—

VIRGINIA: Who cares about the world's opinion? Do we need France's permission to act in our interests?

SUZANNE: But these interests—these interests are oil, these interests are money—

VIRGINIA: You act like going to war for oil is somehow wrong.

SUZANNE: It *is* wrong.

VIRGINIA: We need oil. Countries have been to war for much less.

SUZANNE: Shouldn't we be better than that?

VIRGINIA: How about stability? Would that make you feel better? Less guilt-ridden?

SUZANNE: It's not about making me feel / better.

VIRGINIA: Saddam was unstable and an enemy. Is that a better bedtime story? You probably feel guilty about Israel too—

SUZANNE: Israel is a difficult—

VIRGINIA: No it's *not*. Israel gives us a much needed ally in that region.

SUZANNE: At the expense of the Palestinian people—

VIRGINIA: You think we should abandon the Jewish citizens, is that what you're saying—

SUZANNE: *(Thrown)* That's not—

VIRGINIA: Forget the holocaust—

SUZANNE: My grandfather *died* in the holocaust—

VIRGINIA: Well, haven't your ancestors suffered enough?

SUZANNE: What I'm trying to say—

VIRGINIA: Your parents must be really distressed with your views.

SUZANNE: My parents understand that it's a complicated situation. (I can't believe you're bringing my parents / into this!)

VIRGINIA: Again with the complications! Some things are simple, Suzanne.

SUZANNE: This isn't.

VIRGINIA: Some things are black and white.

SUZANNE: When you do this—this polarization, you create enemies—you *manufacture* them— Look at the war on communism.

VIRGINIA: But we *won* against communism!

SUZANNE: By funding the Taliban. Just like we "won" against Iran by funding Saddam. And now—

VIRGINIA: Our allies changed—

SUZANNE: And now we're funding groups in *Iran* to / overthrow—

VIRGINIA: *Pro*-democracy groups. Why do you hate democracy, Suzanne?

SUZANNE: *(Matching her in tone)* I hate fighting a war against a country that's using weapons I gave them, Virginia.

VIRGINIA: This administration lives in the real world. Alliances change after a betrayal—

SUZANNE: Our actions—

VIRGINIA: Sometimes subtly—

SUZANNE: What we do—

VIRGINIA: You defend yourself against enemies—

SUZANNE: The choices we make—

VIRGINIA: You defend yourself against enemies in the *present*.

SUZANNE: *(A moment of force)* The choices we make in the present have repercussions in the *future*. My husband's death is in fact a repercussion of Bush Senior's Middle East policy in the 80s.

VIRGINIA: Are you blaming the United States for your husband's death?

SUZANNE: *(Confused)* Yes—no— / indirectly—

VIRGINIA: That's crazy.

SUZANNE: I've been to Baghdad with Jeffrey—I've seen the wreckage of the first / Gulf war—

VIRGINIA: Again, "I've seen—"

SUZANNE: But that's all we have—our *experience*.

VIRGINIA: Your experience is not what we are talking / about.

SUZANNE: What are we here to talk about if not my experience? Would anyone care what I had to say if I didn't have the experience of losing my husband?

VIRGINIA: That's *exactly* what I'm *saying*.

SUZANNE: No, you're saying that I don't have the right to say what I *believe*—

VIRGINIA: Without your grief, you'd be just another American.

SUZANNE: And that doesn't give me the right to say what I believe? That's what democracy *means*, / Virginia—

VIRGINIA: No one would *care* what you believe.

SUZANNE: You're right. But ideally, every American should have *this* opportunity. The chance to be *heard* shouldn't only be relegated to a handful of people who look good on T V—

VIRGINIA: Thank you, I'll take that as a compliment.

SUZANNE: Or who *talk* louder than / everyone else—

VIRGINIA: Instead, you have the opportunity to exploit your husband's death. Good for / you.

SUZANNE: How am I exploiting / my husband's—

VIRGINIA: You're using his death as a *platform*.

SUZANNE: A platform for what?!

VIRGINIA: Fame, celebrity.

SUZANNE: *(With scorn)* I get to be on T V? If I could choose between being on T V and having / my *life* back—

VIRGINIA: We have to listen / to you as if you're—

SUZANNE: I *can't* choose— Listen to me! Being a witness, the story changes you.

VIRGINIA: As if you're an expert on pain and / sorrow—

SUZANNE: You want me to become like you, hard and scared—

VIRGINIA: I am *not* scared!

SUZANNE: *(A triumphant realization)* You are—*terrified.* I won't be like that. I won't raise my child to be like that.

VIRGINIA: Do you want to hear about terror? Have you seen the videotape of your husband's murder?

SUZANNE: No, I—

VIRGINIA: I have.
He's crouched on the floor. His hands are shackled in front of him. He is *begging* for his life, crying for mercy. A man with a black hood pulls him by the hair and with the other hand, draws the knife across his throat. Your husband's body falls to the floor while this *monster* holds your husband's head in triumph. The

body of your husband writhes on the floor, still moving as the blood pours from his neck.
That is now part of *my* experience.

(SUZANNE *can barely breathe, can barely speak.*)

SUZANNE: I can't—I can't do this. I don't know why I thought I could.

(SUZANNE *takes off her mike and exits.* VIRGINIA *is speechless. She turns to the camera, searching for words.*)

VIRGINIA: I'm— I'm sorry if I—if I got over-involved but Jeffery Roth's death disturbed me. Greatly. It was a tragedy, I think. A preventable tragedy if only we had been able to hit these—*terrorists* where they live. Before they had the chance. To strike.
We have to go to Charles Jackson in Syria.

(*Graphics. Music.* VIRGINIA *sits, shocked at what just occurred.* JIM *enters.*)

JIM: (*Ironically*) Well, you showed her.

VIRGINIA: I told you I couldn't—

JIM: Take off your goddamn microphone.

VIRGINIA: I told you—

JIM: You're on satellite FEED. You think they stop broadcasting when they say they do—
(*He rips the mike off her dress.*)
What the fuck was that?

VIRGINIA: I told you that there was no way I could win—

JIM: Oh, it's not a matter of winning, Ms Eames. You are so far beyond the idea of winning.

VIRGINIA: You told me to be relentless—

JIM: I didn't tell you to be a freak show! I didn't tell you to describe a snuff film on national T V!

VIRGINIA: So now, you have *morals*?

JIM: Don't make this about me, Virginia. I never told you to—

VIRGINIA: *(Agonized)* "Scare her from getting in the ring", what did you think I was going to do?

JIM: I've been trying to get you your own goddamned show!

VIRGINIA: What?

JIM: Irene's moving to A B C. They need a replacement. And I've been pitching you—God help me.

VIRGINIA: They might still want me for the job. I *deserve* that job.

JIM: Are you thinking of *career advancement* after what you did to that woman?

VIRGINIA: That woman—

JIM: What, she had it coming? No one's gonna see it that way!

VIRGINIA: They will if I tell them to.

JIM: You just lay low—

VIRGINIA: I will not.

JIM: I'm telling you—

VIRGINIA: I will not let her define what happened today!

JIM: Darlin', you got no choice.

VIRGINIA: Book me. On all the shows.

JIM: You won't get anything mainstream.

VIRGINIA: Jim, I don't need the mainstream. I know my audience.

Scene Fourteen
My side:
Pat and Daniel discuss what makes a story and
Virginia tells the truth.

(PAT *and* DANIEL *in his office. Meanwhile, video plays on the monitors:* VIRGINIA *doing interviews, we only see her response. Over the course of the scene, we see four different interviews with four different sets behind her.)*

DANIEL: There isn't a story.

PAT: A conservative mouthpiece loses control on national T V. It's a *great* story.

VIRGINIA: Thanks for having me on, Sean.

DANIEL: The article already went to press, Pat.

PAT: One paragraph. A blip on the radar. It's bigger than that.

VIRGINIA: It's been insane.

DANIEL: Things happen on national T V all the time. At any given time, there are hundreds of channels transmitting information.

VIRGINIA: The way people have overreacted.

PAT: The widow's only interview!

VIRGINIA: I understand her grief, okay?

DANIEL: The owner of this paper owns the publishing company that's putting out Virginia's book. *They're* spinning the story. And *they* only want a paragraph on B3. Read the memo.

(DANIEL *passes the memo to* PAT; *she reads it.)*

VIRGINIA: But the things Ms Roth was saying—

DANIEL: They don't want Virginia to look bad. Okay? You happy?

VIRGINIA: I mean, Ms Roth actually blamed her husband's death on the United States government.

PAT: Run a longer story anyway.

DANIEL: Why would I do that? Why would I throw myself headlong into shit to destroy a young girl's career?

VIRGINIA: Basically, the widow's a whack job.

PAT: Maybe her career should be destroyed.

VIRGINIA: Honestly, Rush, I hope she gets some help.

DANIEL: Why? Because she says some things you don't agree with? She has the right to say what she believes; she has the right!

VIRGINIA: I just feel sorry for her little girl.

PAT: And we have the right to take her down. It's time, Daniel.

VIRGINIA: And all the things the newspapers are saying, they're all quotes taken out of context.

DANIEL: We have real news to report.

VIRGINIA: I mean, if anybody knows how the liberal media distorts what people say, it's *you*, Bill.

PAT: You're still protecting her.

DANIEL: Pat, how many times can we argue about Virginia? I can't do it anymore. This decision is out of my *hands.*

VIRGINIA: I love my country.

PAT: Would you though?

DANIEL: God, Pat, let it GO.

PAT: Would you run a story, a real story—
(She gestures with the memo)
if it weren't for this memo?

DANIEL: What do you want from me?!
You want me to say that I would tear down her career
if they'd let me? I wouldn't. At least when she's on
T V—

PAT: What.

DANIEL: *(Hating himself)* At least when she's on T V, I
get to see her.

VIRGINIA: *(A little teary)* I'm sorry. I love my country
and it's really sad that I have to apologize for that.

(PAT sits down. DANIEL walks to the window.)

PAT: You know, when I first met her, I was so
impressed. The fact that she talked back. The fact that
she had *opinions*, I thought, "She's just like me."

VIRGINIA: Thank God for you guys.

DANIEL: She's not. She's nothing like you.

VIRGINIA: It's been great being on a show where I don't
have to defend myself—

PAT: I know that. I know that now.

VIRGINIA: Where someone's listening to *my side* of the
story.

DANIEL: I thought I could move on. But.

PAT: Don't finish that sentence.

VIRGINIA: *(Coquettishly)* Who needs the Today show,
anyway?

Epilogue
Out of the frame:
A year later, Pat asks Virginia a question.

(A light along the downstage)

(A street, PAT walks past VIRGINIA.)

PAT: Virginia?

VIRGINIA: Oh. Pat.

PAT: I thought that was you.

(Beat)

VIRGINIA: It's me.

PAT: I guess I should say congratulations. The show.

VIRGINIA: Yeah.

PAT: I thought after the—after *The Press Speaks* show a year ago and the—uh—

VIRGINIA: *(Helpfully)* Firestorm in the press?

PAT: Yes. I thought, how's she going to get out of this one. But you do land on your feet, don't you. Your own show.

VIRGINIA: There was an opening. I took it.

PAT: Congratulations. You worked for it.

VIRGINIA: How are things at The Nation?

PAT: I like not being at a daily. Following in your footsteps, I guess.

VIRGINIA: Well, it was nice to—

PAT: How's Daniel?

(Beat)

VIRGINIA: He says he's getting out of the game. I don't know what a newspaperman does when he stops working for a newspaper.

PAT: I guess you'll find out.

VIRGINIA: Things were done between us awhile ago. We just. Went in different directions.
You're still living in New York?

PAT: Yes, I'm just working in town for the month.

VIRGINIA: Well. Then we'll see each other. At the parties.

PAT: Yes. That'll be good. We can share memories of better times.

VIRGINIA: The days at *The Post*?

PAT: Better times, in general.

VIRGINIA: I'm glad you stopped me. It was good to see you.
(She kisses her on the cheek, starts to move on.)

PAT: I have to ask. On the show with the widow.

VIRGINIA: I've already given my mea culpas, Pat—

PAT: When you described Jeffrey Roth's death, you said Jeffrey pitched forward. You said you could see his body writhing.

VIRGINIA: Barbaric.

PAT: I've watched that video over and over again and—

VIRGINIA: Pat, I really have to—

PAT: The video doesn't show Jeffery's body.

VIRGINIA: What?

PAT: He falls out of the frame, after the beheading. What you said on that show. It didn't happen.

VIRGINIA: It did happen.

PAT: You didn't see it. You never saw it.

VIRGINIA: *(With a smile)* Does it matter, Pat. Really. Does it?

(VIRGINIA pats PAT on the hand and walks away into the upstage studio area. PAT stands looking after her. The video monitors flicker on. VIRGINIA's image is on all of them. Lights begin to fade on PAT.)

VIRGINIA: Thank you for joining us.
Tonight, we'll be talking about the ongoing fight
in the Middle East and how the media continues to
undermine our troops, the Bush administration and
most importantly, our country.
I'm Virginia Eames and this is "Point/Counterpoint."

(The lights go out on VIRGINIA. *The video image stays on
the monitors. Beat)*

END OF PLAY

www.ingramcontent.com/pod-product-compliance
Lightning Source LLC
Chambersburg PA
CBHW052202090426
42741CB00010B/2376